red cotton

Published in Tshwane, South Africa, by impepho press in 2018
impephopress.co.za
ISBN 978-0-6399465-0-4

Edited by Robert Berold
Cover and layout by Tanya Pretorius
Proofread by Sarah Godsell

Print production by [•]squareDot Media
Printing by LawPrint

The original version of *red cotton* was written as part of gantsho's Masters theses in Creative Writing at the University Currently Known as Rhodes.

Earlier versions of some poems in this book have appeared in the following websites, literary journals and anthologies: Atlanta Review (2018), Illuminations (2017), New Coin. (2017), New Contrast (2017), To Breathe into Another Voice (2017), Tyhini (2017), Type/Cast (2017), and as a video on Youtube.

red cotton

vangile gantsho

for umama and remembering utata

"When you remember me, my child,
be sure to recall that Mama was
a sinner. Her soul was lost
(according to her mama) the very
first time she questioned God. (It
weighed heavily on her, though she
did not like to tell.)
But she wanted to live and what is more
be happy
a concept not understood before the age
of twenty-one.
She was not happy
with fences"

From *Mississippi Winter II* by Alice Walker

contents

i

ii

i

*

I'm standing in the middle of the road trying to drown out my mother's voice. She tells me I'll go to hell for all the men who come in and out of my bed. She doesn't know about the women. I wonder if there is a worse kind of hell for people like me.

• • •

something frozen catches the wind
whispers a maybe into the rain

chanting-humming far away
a brewing storm of smallgirls coming

    the knot, the blindfold and the maze
    a lonesome table with a plastered leg

• • •

    the same beggar, two rand, without a face
    smallgirl-women playing hopscotch on the roof

• • •

A beautiful brown man in a well-cut navy suit pees onto a dead brown face. I watch as his urine goes into her eyes. I am impressed by his aim.

• • •

When I was young, I watched my mother cut up a skirt. She was crying. She wrote a letter and placed it, with the skirt, into a yellow plastic bag. I followed her to my father's car, where she placed the plastic bag on the driver's seat.

• • •

here, the *hurry, quickly, fix your skirt*
the strings and chalk and morning dew
a friend of a friend who knows someone's friend

• • •

My mother thinks I am a whore. I don't know if I disagree.

• • •

I am ravenous on street corners on a summer day. Taunted by short shorts and perky breasts. An old white woman sits by the window while a waiter serves her a plate of something that could buy bread and fish every day for two weeks at least. She eats two forkfuls.

• • •

In a dream, I am haunted by the shadow of an old man, who may have been my father, or brother. An old man with eyes breathing heavily on me. Ears, expectant, dripping saliva over something lace. Black. Or red, brailed by curly hints of carelessly-trimmed pubic hair. And I lay before him, as if behind a glass window. Offering two mouthfuls.

• • •

a pink cotton invitation under the table
the ill-timed blood on a lover's fingers

the smell of impepho in the middle of the night

. . .

Today there is no black. No dark. No light.
Today there are only blues and blood. Hope and heart.

    a half-done face in a coffin.

a brewing storm of smallgirls coming

*

A girl   a spoon   a large plate
Seven children   each with spoons
Only   she   is   left   hungry

Sis Kookie

When I was three, we lived next to a woman named Sis Kookie.
Mama couldn't understand why I loved her so much.
I would sneak out of the window, or the door, when she wasn't looking.

Sometimes I would disappear into the tides of itoyi-toyi.
Mama learned to keep an ear out for those.
Locked the doors. Closed the windows. Tied me with a towel to her back.
I once followed itoyi-toyi all the way to Leondale
before washing up at the feet of a woman from our neighbourhood.

Sis Kookie would sit me on her waist, serving beer, cracking jokes.
Sometimes she'd place me on a chair in the middle of a conversation
Ask someone to watch me while she went about
fetching something   or breaking up fights.

I think mama was scared someone would touch me.
I never told her the man who collected money at her church
used to kiss me with his mouth open.

Once, Sis Kookie chased out   with an axe
an old man who brought a school girl into her yard.
She slapped the girl and sent her home.
After that, on days when mama had to work,
she would drop me off herself.

sorting beans

i used to sit with my aunts sorting beans
stones mostly   sometimes aborted beans
that now resembled stones
my aunt thought i was wasteful   gave me only half a cup
rinsing samp. eight years old
hiding in a kitchen full of women telling stories
nozuko's dad who never returned
zandile who fell pregnant in secondary school
chopping carrots   peeling potatoes

i could never play with the other children by the river
my tongue did not belong in the water
or these kitchen conversations
asked too many questions, for an eight year old
it swam too easily   floating on its back staring at clouds
showing off its english

grandmother's drawer

there is a brown antique cupboard in my grandmother's house
once locked   with blankets and secrets no one could steal

after she passed   only photographs remained
traces   and   gaps   in the cupboard drawer that no longer locked

my aunt on her graduation day   my youngest uncle turning five   or six
utata standing behind umama in their early twenties

two days before tata's funeral   looking for blankets
mama found herself inside my grandmother's drawer

trying not to cry   for a young woman in a photo
who didn't know then

that the man behind her   would leave
long before he died

*

utata waits for me inside a drum
i cannot reach him   until i peel him off the tractor blades
piece him together   scattered on a maize field
carry him home in a wreath and broken string of white beads

umakhulu warned him   against spilling calamine
playing too close to the river
she hid a drum   inside a kist   in the shed
to protect him
I cannot reach it without red and white beads

*

In grade one, an epileptic fit put me into a coma.
A boy in my class told my father I was dead.

A woman in my mother's church drove into a truck.
She broke her arm. Died two weeks later from other wounds.

A single star led a young man to the blade of a noose.
He choked on his blood and died.

The first time I thought about dying, I was five years old.
My grandfather had a heart attack driving back from school.

When I was twenty two, I walked thirty minutes to the train tracks
in my pyjamas. A train never came.

My box smells of cheap wine and sleeping tears.
This wind whispers *vuma ukufa* into my walls.

smallgirl

smallgirl with moths in her mouth
speaks anger in glances   knows the dagger of words
smallgirl   big voice   moves in silence
knows how earthquakes begin

in the rumbling of her stomach
entire families collapse

smallgirl cares too much   for such a small girl
smallgirl with treacherous eyes
carries too much feeling in her lungs
knows the sting of lonely
smallgirl sees too much   breathes too much
takes up too much air
smallgirl is too much mirror and   expectation
too much wanting more
smallgirl should know better than to try fight the sun

smallgirl with hands of spades
smallgirl dreams too much. hopes too much
wants to plant and grow
smallgirl thinks she is the ocean
smallgirl is a stream

smallgirl will break her heart with all this want
smallgirl is not even the wind

smallgirl must learn to swallow
and be pretty

*

in the face brick house on the hill,
a young man makes a home with ghosts.

he sleeps in a small wing near the gate,
asks their permission to leave every day. and to return.

his girlfriend pulls a patch of hair from his head
every week he denies her their master bedroom.

when he begs the ghosts to move into the house
they hide her shoes in the basement so she cannot leave.

breathing under water

I'm told my grandmother was a woman of the spirit
That the wind carried her off a cliff
Flung her straight into the water
where I was born   wrapped in the skin of a snake

I stayed under water for sixty days before I met my mother
in a burning hut on the mountain
She could enter only to fetch me and put me down
Was allowed only to feed me
then return me to the fire

I'm told my lungs are made of water
That a snake coils around my spine
and I carry hives of bees inside my breasts

They say when a girl becomes a woman
she must leave her mother's house
Not be afraid of the wind and the cliff
She must learn to trust her breath under water

Mama and I have never truly touched
A god of   someone's god   has always kept us apart
Her in her prayers
Me in the water

*

we pass each other   every day   on the streets
carefully hidden behind sunglasses and tight smiles

we are intentional with each other   careful to cover
the bumps and folds of measured bile

weighing each other up against the lumps in our throats
a laugh   a hug   apples in a vase on a white linen cloth

a heavy cigarette stub threatens two leaves
fractured limbs   empty bottles   once-worn shoes

in a storm of secrets   in the middle of the night
a waltzing silence breaks free from a lonely string

*

When I can't - - - - -
I - - - - hangman with utata.

He can - - - - - guess the word.
I am - - - - - - hanging
In imagined - - - -

Locked - - - - - - in my spine
- - - always pining for him
And - - - - always a mirage

*

utata was in court when i was born
by the time he arrived, they had finished sewing mama closed.

mama says i would cry for weeks when tata was away.
she once hiked for three hours in tears to give me to him.
he was in court when we barged in.
mama was too tired to care.

when i turned four and a half
my younger brother was born
he was utata's favourite.
after that i only appeared occasionally,
for long drives and late-night conversation.

mama worked too hard
was always too practical.
never drank whisky.
cried the entire time i was inside her.

sometimes, when mama wasn't working
they would lock themselves in their room for hours.
other than then, tata hardly slept at home.

once, i spent an entire month reading
the two "s" volumes of the encyclopaedia
in case tata wanted us to have a conversation.
my younger brother, even when he was older,
only ever played tv games and watched cartoons.

i have never been able to cut the cord from umama.
i am always swimming too close to her shore.

*

A twelve year old girlchild bleeds for the first time
a year after her mother passes away
She tears a piece off her scarf for the strip of her panties
Her mother never taught her how to sit in her blood

At school the other girls tease her
Her blood is unruly   trickling down her leg
A reused cloth   washed in a basin
She learns to cut legs out of plastic bags

Many cycles later   while giving a lecture
a woman sneezes a large clot of blood onto her panties
She can feel it threaten to spill into her jeans
She still does not know how to bleed in public

When her daughter bleeds for the first time
she is far away
On the phone   she talks her daughter through her cramps
She cannot prepare her   for the many betrayals her blood will bring

*

in a giant waiting room on the beach, hiding between a rock and a wall, a great

white tiger sits on the shore. waiting for me to come towards the water, daring

me almost. her eyes are empty. she tells me she has no name. i understand. she

tells me she's run away from the circus. she was tired then. is worse now. she

wants to sleep. i tell her i'm going to sleep inside a mountain. i'm tired too. the

tiger is hollow, listening to me. she has no roar. i ask her why she is sitting in full

view on the sand. she says she hopes someone will shoot her out of fear.

Mama I am burning

for Fezeka "Khwezi" Kuzwayo

I am burning mama. Mama, I'm burning.

In a box. Set on fire while I slept.

I slept mama.

A girl faced the bullets head on. She caught a bullet in her eye.

She is blind mama.

Something is wrong mama. I kept pulling down my skirt.

Kept checking my lipstick. I was hiding in this box.

They found me hiding mama.

This fire is an uncle you trusted mama.

An uncle who promised to watch me while you were gone.

And while you were gone, in my sleep, the fire burned me mama.

While you were gone.

While I was sleeping.

I forgot to pull my skirt down. I put too much lipstick on.

I am burning mama. Mama, I am burning!

*

smallgirl sleeps next to her mother
two   new   moons   that never touch
mother is always holding her breath
even in her sleep
smallgirl rubs calamine onto mother's eyelids
plaits three   five   seven
white beads into mother's hair
when mother awakes
smallgirl is snaked around her spine

taxi ride

he owns the pavement
he owns the street
he owns everyone in the taxi
the taxi driver owns my thighs
I focus on remembering my multiples of twelve

a young woman with a baby on her lap gets out
an older woman castigates her
for having two children so young
the taxi driver hoots for a replacement
struggles to get out of first gear
he has a beguiling smile
his hands are sandpapering through my dress

a sea of children in school uniform
follow the FEES MUST FALL protesters
the taxi driver says he is proud of these young people
the sandpaper reaches for the ashtray in between my legs
he is looking for change

at a bus stop an old man is waiting for his taxi to fill up
he throws me a wanton smile
a passing car belts out: *iqgirha le ndlela*

a thick Xhosa accent thunders to the front of the taxi
the older woman mumbles something
this is followed by a conversation on grants
everyone speaks over the other
everyone has an opinion
everyone knows someone who is on some kind of grant
the grey-haired man is ogling my chest
the gear stick makes one last attempt on my thighs

*

A friend of a friend tells me of a woman who held her dying lover to her belly.
His last breath was a kiss to their unborn child.
Two days later, she followed him out of the window from the fifteenth floor.

• • •

Our house is burning   the women in green and black are dancing.
They throw their panties to fuel the fire.
Offer their breasts and thighs as a singing sacrifice.

• • •

uSno once walked all the way from the tar road to my grandmother's house with a baby on her back.
She didn't know he was dead until she untied the towel to find something cold.

• • •

A ten year old boy rapes a seven year old girl. The other children watch with their phones. No one will
want to see when she washes the blood with calamine.

• • •

There is a scar the length of my hand that extends from my pelvis to my thigh
Every time it begins to heal, I pick at it in my sleep.

• • •

A man who raised three children pins his helper to the floor.
The woman who raised his children walks in as he unzips his pants.
On the phone, the helper's words sound like a sharp knitting needle
into the daughter's head. Down her neck.
A razor blade cuts a hole into her heels. To bury the secret.

• • •

My sister has baked four cakes in her life
Only one has ever made it out the oven.

• • •

I wake up to the sound of cockroaches plotting against me.
All over my floors. Inside my cupboards.   Building an army.
I burn impepho   locked up in my bathroom.
A cockroach crawls out of my vagina.

*

tata's voice grows louder, shouting at umama for not making me stronger. everything sounds louder. mama's crying now. praying. i beg the tiger to hide behind the bed with me. we can go and sleep in the mountain together. "i can't protect you if you're so exposed." tata's drunk now. mama's trying to stop him from coming to my room. the tiger moves so slowly! she doesn't want to be saved. and i am too heavy. too heavy to fetch her.

the flush

a young girl obsesses about calories and food
she struggles to swallow a pea
the skin between her eyes and cheek bones
reminds me of my cousin born at six months
later   when they sedate her
before she passes out   she begs the nurse to not make her fat
she looks at me   swallows something   vomit maybe

in the dining hall   i sit at a table   alone at the back
we're forced to eat before taking our medication
a tall man with black pits for eyes sits opposite me
a short anxious woman with a pierced eyebrow follows him
she asks if i have cigarettes   i do
black pits asks me to come watch him play basketball

i don't attend any of the group therapy sessions
my therapist tells me about bipolar
i swop my anti-depressants for sleeping pills   with a woman from dorm three
black pits comes to fetch me   forces me to watch him play basketball
he pulls my covers off   finds a dress in my locker   undresses me

when mama arrives   it's past visiting hours
her look of jetlag and panic dares the nurses to protest
it's my second week in here   they call it *the flush*
they sedate me for the weekend   to flush out the sleeping pills
mama washes me while i sleep   always   she prays
when looking for my panties   she finds a box of cigarettes in my drawer
she shouts at my sleeping body   for all the ways I try to die

schizophrenia

some definitions

a serious mental illness in which a woman forces her ten year old daughter to wash in a river during winter for buying sweets with her two cents change.

a psychotic disorder characterised by a fifteen year old girl trying to calm her mother from attacking a baby she believes is the devil on a bus. also known as *inherited paranoia*.

the co-existence of opposing voices. example, *she may cook and sew curtains as service, but may not serve as a leader because she is divorced – Assemblies of God.*

*

Mama tells me about two cuts between her thumb and her forefinger.
She visited a doctor for the first time when she was in boarding school.
until then, there was always utamkhul'uSolomzi for the body
umakhul'uNoMhatu for the head
uJwarha for special requests. She was said to collect bats' wings in a jar.

There were always bones and stones and camphor.
Plants brewed into teas, ointments pounded out of bark.
The river was for more than washing and water
the mountain carried just as many secrets, and boys.
The river was also where the girls were sometimes lost.

Mama has never mentioned these scars until now.
She tells me to pick a spoon from a peach tree to stir the medicine with.
To speak into the bucket on a straw mat next to my bed.
I have a list of her and utata's ancestors on a page on the wall.
A white candle on a white cloth on my left. A purple candle on my right.
Mama tells me to pour one cup into two litres of water ndizokugaba,
the rest will be spoken under a blanket over a two-plate stove.
Iyeza will sweat umthakathi out of my body.
I will see a face, or hear a name
but before I do

Mama asks that we pray.
And though she hands me over to abaphantsi, she pleads
with God to keep me close
She doesn't cry, out loud. But I can hear from her voice, she is scared.
She does not know if I will ever come back to her
Once I have seen what they can do for me.

*

an old bride who paid her own lobola
the wayward aunt with a nip and a bible
the cousin who stared a little too much when we bathed

i know now how tata felt
trapped under unflinching expectation
a butterfly with broken limbs in a jar

here   there are blooming weeds   blossoming lava
the nose at the foot of the journey
the curse my grandmother dreamt

disappearing

I know nothing of wars but I imagine they all begin with Jack falling down the hill and breaking his crown and Jill coming tumbling after.

• • •

Red or blue? When I can't decide, I pull the petals off an imaginary daisy to avoid the disappointment in utata's eyes.

• • •

I tell my niece she's a fire princess. She's excited … In years to come, someone she loves will turn her into embers. Then leave her for something more flammable.

• • •

The day I turn twenty one, my brothers each grab one of my feet. Plant me deeply into a sister-bed and cover me with soil. When I detach myself from my legs, mama covers my vagina with a cloth her uncle gave her when she was twelve years old. She tells me to keep it covered until I meet my husband.

• • •

I am always aware of my weight. Always too heavy. And sometimes I disappear completely.

• • •

I wish I'd waited a few hours before falling asleep. My eyeliner only magnifies my swollen eyes. Umama says the world shouldn't see your roof caving in. Not until they enter your house.

• • •

My girlfriend hates penetration. Her fingers are always careful not to go too deep into me. When I go down on her, I nibble on her clit while rubbing the rim of her vagina with a pink vibrating egg. When she raises her pelvis, I slip it in. I can feel her grip tighten as I try to slip my fingers out. This is the first time I've dared to enter her walls.

*

I am the back of these street palms   lines drawn from thirst

wrapped in a chitenge.

I have no reason.   No excuse.   Nothing wounded.

Just a woman who walks freely into men.

And women.

I walk into cars   and arms   and legs.

I walk into motels on some nights.

Or back alleys.

My body knows walking.

Feet   hands   penises.

Knows people less.

My body is nothing worth remembering.

Nothing worth keeping.   Or taking home.

On the streets

I am a vagina, for walking in and out of.

a smallgirl guide for wayward women

be a witch
a temptress
be free
in love
and sex
have lots of sex

smear yourself
all over their bibles
stain their linen
with your cum

be wild
speak out of turn
throw your head back in laughter
sit with your legs open
let the wind kiss
your lady
wink
she's no lady

flirt with the first person you see
reek of sex
smell your fingers
taste them
let her scent sit
on your upper lip
enjoy the throbbing
of his pumping
in a queue at the bank
make the teller envy you
let out an "Ah!"
throw your head back in laughter

spit and gravy

tanci asks me to sew the button onto his jacket
he's going through a divorce

he beat uncinci for years before she kicked him out
no one said anything because he works for the unions

one night, mama washed ncinci's face with dettol while she cried
i went to school in the morning, left ncinci sleeping in my bed

eventually, tanci pulled a gun on her in a whisky-rage
he pulled the trigger, but it wasn't loaded

ncinci is still at home with my cousins
tata told tanci he could stay with us

last night i spat in his plate. stirred it into his gravy.
i use red cotton to sew the navy button onto his jacket

*

My baby cousin turns five.

At her birthday party, her best friend keeps crying. He also wants a cake.

My baby cousin decides to turn him invisible. Handcuffs him to her.

On the jumping castle, they hold hands. Synchronise their jumps.

Every time someone else tries to talk to her, he farts.
Then bursts out laughing.
Nobody can hear him but her.

She shouts at him, embarrassed. She can't remember how to make him visible again.

All the adults smile politely and ask her to excuse herself next time.
The other children pull faces at her. Tell her not to come too close.

When it's time, they blow out her candles together. Her mother cuts two slices of cake.

*

Say you're a fish

Say you love me

Say you're not afraid

Plant yourself into my sand

Follow me into the ocean

Let me swallow you

Say you're a fish

*

Everyone is a pathway to me
A door you cannot bring yourself to open.

There is a darkness in you I walk willingly into
The look you give me when you smoke by my window
The way you stare and scrunch your face slightly without knowing
I wish you were blindfolded most times
That I could exist without the judgment of your eyes
You see too much of me. There is too much of me for you to see
And I worry you don't like me
That you don't love yourself enough to love me

So I lead you to tamer versions of me
Prettier women. Smaller. Less talkative.

the day you left

the day you left
the trees wept all their leaves
in a week, the grass grew pale
my chest turned into a starless sky
i refused to cry for you
not a single tear

i had been gone long before

the winter came
you could not bring yourself to believe it
all your tears, turned green
flowers by your riverbank

i was an abandoned hut waiting
a roof
a door
anything to make a home
i imagined housing your laughter
you rolling around inside me

surely you must have known

you were always something in the meantime

a place to rest on my way to the city
bright lights and skyscrapers

you wanted noise
i made you think too much

you hoped i would return

i knew you knew, i would not

sleeping next to you

I am sleeping next to you.
I know by your breathing how far away you are.

Your mouth twitches slightly, every time you inhale.
My feet are sometimes brave. Reach out to yours.
Never arrive.   But try

You are able to travel   in my bed.
Escape to somewhere
far away from me.

In your bed   and mine
I clench my body into silence.
All my movements are heavy, even when blinking

I am afraid of waking you.
I never exhale.
I cannot risk us breathing over each other.

I can tell you the exact moment we broke.
I watched you see me find an empty box under your bed.
You didn't explain. You were gone by then.

I searched for you frantically.
Found you in a torn latex wrapper in the dustbin.

Found you in a bite mark on your arm.
A stray scent.
A spiteful strand of hair.

ii

the corner of our ceiling

There is a room in the house we share
That neither of us may enter
We had not noticed it before, when we used to talk
Now the silence rattles the door
A gentle back and forth against the frame while we sleep

Inside

A pair of black gumboots covered in mud

Soils a brown carpet with a single stain

A dark patch, blood or ink maybe, in the middle of the room

A half-burned candle melted into an empty jar of baby food

The wind has scattered snuff all over the floor

A vase with dead flowers on a small side-bed table

No bed

We blame the silence for the room
The door we cannot open
We share a bed on which we never touch
Our roof leaks. We do not fix it
The mould on the corner of our ceiling
Is the only conversation this house knows

*

a dead baby waits for a woman by a door
wrapped in a yellow blanket.

the woman takes the baby home.
nurses it for three days,
before planting it in her garden.

it has been three years since she lost her son.
the half-crescent scar below her stomach has almost disappeared.

a pink rose the size of a small tree now grows
from where her baby was planted.

the scar

i remember you the way my body carries the scar on my neck. a virus that ate at my lymph nodes for months before the doctors knew what it was. they had to cut a hole into my neck to find it. you were not as kind. for years, i nursed a gaping hole... vodka-filled... trying to... something you out of me... anything you out... you were everywhere... in me... spread heavy into my feet... burning in my thighs... i want to remember you before... the gaping... the paralysis... before the cutting... but it's almost too distant... running through a mall... screaming... throwing ourselves on the floor... little children on the playground... there were kisses... you lost my favourite sunglasses. there was always something with you... with us... me introducing you to my best friend... you being too high to be polite. you catching a bus to my father's funeral... me finding a pair of panties under your bed.

i have to remind myself not to miss... that i would sit for hours in the dark... unable to move... to think... unable to cry... that you are a scar somewhere... i cannot touch.

green scarf

in the laundromat
a full dark woman rummages
dirty clothes
the purple hoodie i slept in
when i heard my father had passed
twice-worn t-shirts, a grey bra
a green scarf i haven't worn in years

it wrapped loosely around me
the morning you left
you refused to hold me
rinsed me off with an iciness
i was sure would shatter me
that scarf held me together
i don't know how it got in here today

*

two beautiful men push me onto a bed. one puts his knees on my wrists and covers my mouth. the other puts his knees on my ankles and unzips his pants. the man on my wrists shoves his tongue down my throat. the unzipped man pulls my panties down my legs. he is a tree stub inside me. with roots tying my legs to the ground. it's his tongue inside my mouth now. maybe i am the ground. and he isn't digging. maybe he's trying to pull his roots out of me. pulling. and pulling. and pulling. maybe he's stuck inside me. the man on my wrists has a gun to my head. he rubs it against my hair, grunting. he is now unzipped. the tree stub is on my wrists. all i feel is the first shot. everything else is him moving. and breathing. and licking the tears down the side of my face. when i close my eyes, i look for god. where is she? i tell her i'm sorry. and i promise to be happier. and drink less. and i won't talk to strangers, no matter how good looking they are. and if she can't make them stop, i beg her to let me sleep. she doesn't let me sleep. she makes me the ground again. with a tree stuck between my legs. and again, i'm shot. and wake up on a patch of red.

*

uMakazi was raised by nuns who told her she was a wicked child for bleeding all over her sheets and bringing them, bloodied, to show Sister MarySomething – surely she should have known blood must always be washed away; like the night Thabiso and Akho spent taking turns digging into me; or when I was five playing house with twelve year old Akhumzi, he put his hand in between my legs because he said that's what his father did to his mother, that I was supposed to make funny moaning sounds; and umama telling me that her principal in secondary school had often told her she had beautiful breasts; and that when he was in form two, umalume came back boasting that he was a man now after an extra maths class with MamXola – at MamXola's funeral, there were rumours that the drunk uncle in the maroon tie used to take MamXola to his room after supper to give her isweets. When I was six, mama told me to sit with my legs closed otherwise men would hurt me.

• • •

*

My lover's nipples meet me affectionately,

a wound my body had not known it missed.

I am caged in her. And she is home.

I am with her. And I am with him.

The three of us   rolling under covers

on a three-quarter mid-morning bed.

We laugh. Tickle. Hands stroking.

Feeling out   where we bleed into each other.

She does not know he is here.

He touches her.

She does not know that we are three.

Or four. Or five.

That we bleed into many, sometimes

• • •

Mama says the nuns made uMakazi carry two planks of wood
to separate her when sitting next to men on the bus
– the nuns said it would prevent her from falling into sin.

She tells me she was eighteen when she rode in the back of a van, alone
with umakhulu's dead body   all the way from Johannesburg to
Queenstown. Tamkhulu couldn't get leave from the mines.

• • •

I don't speak to umama anymore

except when I tell her of fictional stories about friends.

I tell her a girl I know was raped by her boyfriend

while visiting him in East London

ten months after being raped by two strangers.

(This girl doesn't drink or smoke and goes to church every Sunday.)

• • •

Another time, I tell her about another girl,

who came back crying after a date in grade eleven with a boy who is now a lawyer.

They drank raw shots of Absolut Vodka in solidarity

and cried together on the stairs in hostel,

(but I don't tell mama the part about the vodka

because she wouldn't understand.)

fresh sheets

I like to pick up men in bars.

Preferably older, with silver hairs and traces of smiling women on their fingers.

I watch their hands. How their mouths take in their whisky.

When they're home... always my home... I smear them all over my sheets. On my walls. Round patches of sweat. Palms. The back of heads.

After, I offer a drink. Place their shoes by their feet.

I collect sheets. Flakes of dry skin. Stray hairs... in a box on my shelf.

The following night, if the moon hangs lonely, I empty the box into a burning bowl of impepho. Prepare a cup of coffee. Change my sheets. Apply my lipstick.

• • •

Mama says her aunt once sent om'nye umakazi wam back to umakhulu
because she said umakazi was trying to break up her home.

Umakhulu let it slip to umama nomakazi
that *her* mother had sent *her* to her aunt
because her father had decided to make her his second wife.

After telling them this mama says umakhulu fetched two basins full of
water
and forced umama nomakazi to wash their lady parts
with a whole bar of green soap until it was finished.

She prayed for, mama says, two hours
asking God
to cleanse her children,
not to let them suffer for the sins of their parents.
And to preserve her family's name.

*

an old woman whispers into a smallgirl's navel
then wraps her neck with red and white beads
the old woman smears calamine on the smallgirl's forehead
under her left breast, between her shoulder blades
when the smallgirl wakes up, her eyes are glued together with tears
she learns to see in the dark
the smallgirl can smell the rain coming
she knows a storm is brewing

a woman tries to rescue her daughter from a burning shack
all the shacks around her are on fire
she hunches herself over her daughter, carries all of her inside
by the time she reaches the tar road, the woman's dress has been burnt to her skin
her daughter survives unharmed
pulls a bottle of calamine out of her pocket
uses a piece of her own dress to dress her mother's wounds
she wraps a string of red and white beads around her mother's waist
whispers into her navel, a secret   about a match

#lessonsfrommymother

1. For children who prefer to hide under beds reading instead of playing, there will always be a sandwich and a glass of milk for company.

2. I will never be too old for a belt over the knee, or a public scolding.

3. Make-up and a pretty dress may not fix anything, but they make great armour.

4. When things feel out of control, there are always clothes to be washed, and cleaning that to be done.

5. After a certain age, brothers and sisters shouldn't share towels.

6. In case you are hit by a car while crossing the street, always make sure you wear good underwear.

7. Sometimes, all you need to feed a family and keep your house is fifty rand and a prayer.

8. Do not ever let a man go through your handbag. Especially if you love him.

9. A woman should know how to take off her bra without taking off her clothes.

10. Quiet is not always silence.

11. Everyone tries the perfume out on their skin, but no man wants to buy the bottle labelled "tester".

12. Some children need to be burnt to know for themselves that the stove is hot.

13. In your house, you must always have toilet paper, soap, toothpaste and a can of pilchards.

*

after Xidu Heshang "Fictionalising Her"

At thirteen, she and her younger brother are living with their father in East London. It takes four taxis for them to make their way home from school. If they find their father's car in the driveway, she takes her brother to watch a movie. Sometimes they walk around the mall eating ice-cream. When they are home, she cooks supper, goes through her brother's homework, makes sure he is washed and put to bed. Her father calls her lazy for not wanting to wake up in the mornings.

In grade eleven, after she's made deputy headgirl, her friends use her key to sneak out of hostel. She threatens to report them if they do it again. They accuse her of not wanting them to get a good education. At meals, they sit in a group hurling deliberate stares at her and sometimes giggling. She stops eating. And leaving her room. She hears them call her an attention-seeker outside her window.

By the time she turns twenty, she has been to two psychiatric homes. The second time, for a conversation with a white tiger on the beach.

When she is twenty one, she is raped by two men. She falls pregnant. Her fear of an ugly child with two violent fathers leads her to a woman in downtown Jo'burg. She replaces her fear with a lie she tells her lovers years later: she's not the kind of woman who wants to be tied down with children.

She drops out of school for the third time when she is twenty four. Her father drops her off with her mother. Says he doesn't want to see her again, until she goes back to school. He drives off without saying goodbye. Six months later, he dies in an accident.

At twenty five, she gets her heart broken for the first time. She doesn't leave until she's twenty six. At twenty six she dates a married man. Then a woman. Then convinces herself she has stopped looking for her father in everyone she meets.

At thirty two, she finds him in a man who refuses to love her.

clots of blood

after Hiromi Itō "Coyote"

My grandmother was a teacher
My mother was a healer
My mother's younger sister was a Christian
My mother's other younger sister had a paralysed daughter
All were wonderfully beautiful.

When I was born, my grandmother sent a telegram with my name.
She saw me in a dream.
My grandmother saw herself reborn through my mother.
When I left home, after she had died
She visited me in a dream.
Painted three dots from blood onto my forehead.

My mother birthed four children.
Her second son took too much of her blood into his heart.
When my brother died in her arms
My mother could not heal him.
When I was born, two years after, my mother had stopped healing.
All her faith clotted inside my lungs.
I didn't cry when I was born.
My mother held me silent, for thirty minutes in her arms.
When the nurse tried to pry me away from her,
My grandmother's telegram arrived.
My mother says I laughed when the nurse tried to take me from her.
She birthed two children after failing to heal her second son.

My mother was a believer.
My grandmother was a healer.
My mother's younger sister was a Christian.
My mother's other younger sister had a paralysed daughter.
All were wonderfully beautiful.

My mother's younger sister's paralysed daughter died when she was fifteen.
My mother's younger sister visited her on the other side.
When her daughter returned,
after three months inside a mechanical heart beat
she had three clots of blood down the front of her body,
On her chest, in her navel, just above her vagina.
She still could not walk.

My grandmother was touched by her father's younger brother.
My mother was touched by her mother's sister's husband.
My mother's younger sister was also touched by her mother's sister's husband.
My mother's other younger sister was touched by her mother's uncle.
My mother had always wanted a daughter.
She never left me alone with any of her sisters' husbands.

The protection my mother gave me
Was The Bible, fear and chastity.
We were all afraid of God, men, and the dark.

*

there is an old woman across the river.
she is made of sand and fire, carrying a child on her back.

i cannot reach her   she has burned the river dry.
the mud is buried   turned angry   swallows rocks

and children   who still believe in water.
it has not rained in three full moons.

smallgirl is no longer a child. the old woman
does not break her back carrying her.

she carried rocks and built a house in another life.
smallgirl is singing. tears are falling from her eyes.

she is tired. her feet do not know the ground.
i tell the old woman to sit her into the river.

smallgirl's feet will bring peace
between the burning sandwoman and the water.

glossary

abaphantsi	ancestors
chitenge	cloth used by women to wrap around their bodies (Malawi)
igqirha le ndlela	"the click song" by Miriam Makeba
itoyi-toyi	Zimbabwean-South African dance used in protests, particularly pre-'94
iyeza	(traditional) medicine
lobola	bride price
(u)/(no)makazi	aunt – mother's sister
(u)makhulu	grandmother
(u)malume	uncle – mother's brother
(i)mpepho	wild chamomile indigenous to sub- Saharan Africa often used (dried and burned) as incense or to help communicate with ancestors
(u)mthakathi	bewitcher
(u)ncinci	aunt – father's younger brother's wife
ndizokugabha	"so I can vomit" (not interchangeable with "throw up" when part of a traditional practice)
om'nye umakazi wam	"another aunt of mine" – mother's sister
(u)tanci	uncle – father's younger brother
(u)tata	father
(u)ta'mkhulu	grandfather
vuma ukufa	agree to die OR acknowledge death

acknowledgments

ndibulela uMdali wam. ndibulele amaYirha, ooDlomo (ooHlanga), amaCirha namaNdungwana. Camagu.

to Robert, thank you for your fine comb and immeasurable generosity. thank you for forcing me to write. for being firm and gentle, and always, for the poetry. i love you dearly.

Tolu Agbelusi, Tanya Pretorius, Dolla Sapeta, Zoya Mabuto and Sarah Godsell, thank you for reading and rereading. Mthunzikazi Mbungwana, thank you for holding.

to my family, those given to me and those i have been blessed with along the way, thank you, thank you, thank you! i am, because you are.

Camagu.

impepho press

Printed in the United States
By Bookmasters